We Use Fire

by Yara S. Mignon

Table of Contents

Chapter 1
Using Fire

Life without fire would not be fun. You would eat <u>raw</u> food. You would not see **fireworks** at celebrations. And camping trips would be boring.

<u>raw</u>: not cooked

Fire can be dangerous. But it is also very useful.

People use fire every day. Sometimes they use fire without knowing it!

⟳ People use fire to cook outdoors.

Chapter 2
Fire at Home

Some people have a fireplace at home. A fireplace can burn wood, gas, or <u>coal</u>. Some fireplaces can be turned on with a button!

<u>coal</u>: a black rock that burns easily

⟳ A fireplace can warm a home.

⌂ When you use a gas stove, flames come out of the burners.

People also use fire at home to cook. Many kitchen stoves use gas. Other stoves use **electricity**. Electric burners turn red to tell you when they are hot. You will not see flames.

In the past, people used fireplaces to heat water. Today, fire still heats water. Now it's easy. You just turn on a faucet when you need hot water.

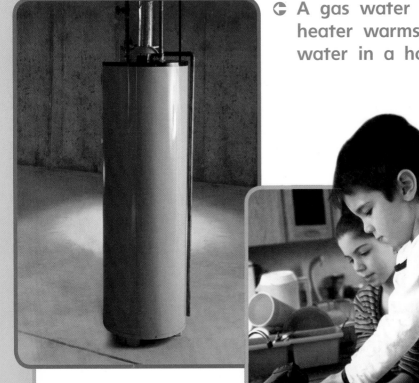

⤺ A gas water heater warms water in a home.

Hot water from ⤵ a faucet has gone through the water heater.

⌂ People used candles at night until the light bulb was invented in 1879.

In the past, people burned candles, oil, or gas to make <u>light</u>. Today we use electricity, and light shines from light bulbs.

Ⓛanguage DETECTIVE

Light: Find *light* three more times on this page.

Chapter 3
Fire at Work

You may not see it, but you use fire to light and heat your home. Fire can be used to make electricity. Electricity can be made by burning coal, gas or oil at a power plant.

⟳ When electricity is made at a power plant, a lot of smoke blows out.

⋒ This person uses fire to make glass vases.

People also use fire to make glass. Hot fires melt sand into glass.

Workers in <u>factories</u> use fire to make things. Metals, like gold, silver, and iron, are taken out of a rock called ore. Then the metals are heated until they melt.

<u>factories</u>: buildings where things are made

↑ Some cooks bake pizza in ovens heated by burning wood.

A regular oven can <u>take</u> one hour to bake breads and pizzas. However, a pizza oven is very hot and can bake quickly. It can cook a pizza in 10 minutes!

Language DETECTIVE

<u>Take</u>: *Take* has the long *a* sound and an *e* at the end. Find another word with the long *a* sound and an *e* at the end on this page and on page 9.

Welders use fire to connect pieces of metal. They use a burner called a **blowtorch**. This makes the metal pieces soft. Then the welder can shape the metal and press it together.

⟳ Welders wear helmets to protect their faces.

Chapter 4
Fire Outdoors

A campfire can keep you warm and cook your food.

Put the fire out before you go home. If you do not, the fire may <u>spread</u>.

<u>spread</u>: to become bigger and go to more places

⬆ You can cook over a campfire.

Forest fires can kill plants and animals. But sometimes fires help the forest.

Thick weeds and grasses can grow over other plants. Also, some seeds can only grow after a fire. Forest **rangers** may set fires. This lets new plants grow.

⏷ Only rangers can set forest fires.

Fire gives us a lot of things—heat, hot water, and even fireworks on the 4th of July!

Fire is powerful. Be safe when you use fire.

 Language DETECTIVE

Exclamation mark !: An exclamation mark ! is used at the end of a sentence to show surprise or strong feeling. Find two more sentences with an exclamation mark ! at the end.

⊕ Fireworks are used on the 4th of July in New York City.

Glossary

blowtorch a burner with a very hot, small flame *(page II)*

electricity a form of energy *(page 5)*

fireworks firecrackers that burn or explode to make a show of light and loud noises *(page 2)*

rangers people who take care of the forest *(page 13)*

welder someone who joins pieces of metal together by heating them *(page II)*

Index

Comprehension Check

Retell

Complete the Main Idea and Details Chart with your class. Then retell the information in this book.

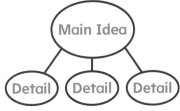

Think and Compare

1. Look at page 6. How do homes get hot water today? *(Identify Main Idea and Details)*

2. Do you think your family could live for one week without heat and fire? Explain. *(Apply)*

3. "Fire is both a friend and a foe." (A foe is an enemy.) Do you think this is true? Explain. *(Evaluate)*